Easy Guide
MySQL

Practical Guide

V. Telman

Practical Guide

1.Introduction

Database management systems (DBMS) are essential in modern computing environments. They allow organizations and developers to manage and organize vast amounts of data efficiently. Among these systems, MySQL has emerged as one of the most popular open-source relational database management systems. This introduction will explore what MySQL is, how to install it, and provide an overview of its architecture. Later, we will dive into getting started with MySQL, including connecting to the system, using the MySQL Command Line Interface (CLI), and understanding MySQL Workbench.

What is MySQL?

MySQL is an open-source relational database management system (RDBMS) that is based on Structured Query Language (SQL), a standard language for managing relational databases. Developed by Oracle Corporation, MySQL is commonly used in web applications, embedded systems, and data processing applications due to its speed, reliability, and flexibility.

MySQL operates as a server, allowing multiple clients to access and manage data concurrently. The data is stored in tables that consist of rows and columns, where rows represent records and columns represent attributes of those records. MySQL is particularly known for its ease of use, extensive documentation, and active community support.

Some key features of MySQL include:

- **Cross-Platform:** MySQL runs on various operating systems, including Windows, Linux, and macOS, making it a versatile choice for developers.
- **High Performance:** MySQL is optimized for speed and can handle large volumes of data efficiently.
- **Scalability:** The database can grow with the needs of an application, and it supports complex queries even as the dataset expands.
- **Security:** MySQL offers various tools

and features for securing sensitive data, including user authentication and SSL encryption.
- **Support for Transactions:** MySQL supports ACID-compliant transactions, ensuring data integrity and reliability.
- **Extensive Community and Resources:** As a widely used open-source solution, MySQL benefits from a large community that provides plugins, extensions, and tools.

Installing MySQL

Installing MySQL is a straightforward process, but it can vary slightly depending on the operating system. Below, we will cover the installation steps for both Windows and Linux environments.

Installing MySQL on Windows

1. **Download MySQL Installer:**
   - Visit the official MySQL website (https://dev.mysql.com/downloads/) and navigate to the MySQL Community Server section.
   - Choose the appropriate MySQL Installer

for your Windows version (either MSI or ZIP format).

2. **Run the Installer:**
   - Open the downloaded installer and select the setup type. The recommended type for most users is "Developer Default," but you can choose "Server only" for a more minimal installation.

3. **Select Components:**
   - On the components screen, you can choose which MySQL components you want to install. The default settings are appropriate for most users, including server, client, documentation, and sample databases.

4. **Configure MySQL Server:**
   - In the configuration settings, you can choose the server configuration type (e.g., development, production). You will also set the root password and optionally create user accounts.

5. **Start the MySQL Server:**
   - After configuration, the installer will install the MySQL server and start it. You can

also choose to have it run as a Windows service.

6. **Complete the Installation:**
   - Follow the prompts to complete the installation, and once finished, you can launch the MySQL Command Line Client or MySQL Workbench.

Installing MySQL on Linux

For Linux users, installation primarily involves using the package manager for your distribution. Below is an example for Debian-based systems (like Ubuntu) and Red Hat-based systems (like CentOS).

For Debian-based Systems (Ubuntu):

1. **Update Package Index:**
   ```bash
   sudo apt update
   ```

2. **Install MySQL Server:**
   ```bash
   sudo apt install mysql-server
   ```

```
```

3. **Secure MySQL Installation:**
   After installation, you can run a security
script to improve MySQL's security settings:
   ```bash
   sudo mysql_secure_installation
   ```

   Follow the prompts to set the root password
   and remove anonymous users.

4. **Start MySQL Service:**
   MySQL service should be started
   automatically, but you can check its status or
   start it manually:
   ```bash
   sudo systemctl status mysql
   ```

5. **Connect to MySQL Server:**
   Once MySQL is installed, you can connect
   to the server using:
   ```bash
   mysql -u root -p
   ```

For Red Hat-based Systems (CentOS):

1. **Enable MySQL Repository:**
   ```bash
   sudo yum
   localinstall https://dev.mysql.com/get/mysql8
   0-community-release-el7-1.noarch.rpm
   ```

2. **Install MySQL:**
   ```bash
   sudo yum install mysql-server
   ```

3. **Start MySQL Service:**
   ```bash
   sudo systemctl start mysqld
   ```

4. **Get Temporary Password:**
   After installation, MySQL generates a temporary password for the root user that you can find in the logs.
   ```bash
   grep 'temporary password'
   /var/log/mysqld.log
   ```

5. **Run Security Script:**
   Secure your installation as mentioned previously for Debian-based systems.

Overview of MySQL Architecture

Understanding MySQL's architecture is crucial for developers and administrators to maximize the system's performance. The architecture includes several layers:

1. **MySQL Server Layer:**
   The MySQL server layer handles all database management tasks, including processing queries, managing connections, enforcing security, and maintaining data. It consists of several sub-components:
   - **Storage Engines:** MySQL supports multiple storage engines (such as InnoDB, MyISAM) that define how data is stored, indexed, and retrieved. InnoDB is the default engine, known for its transactional support and data integrity.
   - **Query Processor:** This component interprets SQL queries and optimizes them for execution. The MySQL optimizer evaluates various execution plans to determine the most

efficient way to process a query.

- **Connection Manager:** This handles incoming client connections and manages sessions, including user authentication.

2. **Storage Layer:**
The storage layer is responsible for storing data in the filesystem. Data is organized into files based on the selected storage engine. For example, InnoDB stores data in tablespace files, while MyISAM uses separate files for each table.

3. **Client Layer:**
The client layer represents the various client applications that connect to the MySQL server. This can include command-line tools, programming language libraries, and graphical user interfaces like MySQL Workbench.

4. **Communication Layer:**
MySQL uses a client-server architecture where client applications communicate with the server over TCP/IP or Unix sockets. The communication layer is responsible for handling incoming requests and sending

responses back to the clients.

Each of these layers interacts with one another to enable efficient data management and access. Understanding this architecture helps developers fine-tune their queries and optimize database performance.

Getting Started

Once MySQL is installed, you can start interacting with your database. This section will cover connecting to MySQL, using the MySQL Command Line Interface (CLI), and getting to know MySQL Workbench.

Connecting to MySQL

After installation, you need to establish a connection to the MySQL server. You can do this using different clients, but we'll focus on the MySQL CLI and MySQL Workbench.

Connecting via MySQL Command Line Interface

1. **Open your terminal or command

prompt.**
2. **Use the following command to connect to the MySQL server:**

```bash
mysql -u username -p
```

Replace `username` with your MySQL username (usually "root" for initial access). After entering the command, you will be prompted to enter your password.

3. **Upon successful connection, you will see a MySQL prompt (`mysql>`), indicating that you're ready to execute SQL queries.**

Connecting via MySQL Workbench

1. **Launch MySQL Workbench.**
2. **Create a new connection by clicking on the `+` icon next to "MySQL Connections."**
3. **Fill in the connection details:**
   - Connection Name: A descriptive name for your connection.
   - Hostname: `localhost` if running on the same machine.

- Port: Default is 3306.
- Username: Your MySQL username (e.g., root).

4. **Click on "Test Connection" to verify that your settings are correct.**
5. **Once confirmed, click "OK" to save the connection. You can now double-click this connection to connect to your MySQL server.**

MySQL Command Line Interface

The MySQL CLI is a powerful tool for executing SQL commands and managing databases. It offers a straightforward command-line interface to interact directly with the MySQL server. Here are some basic commands you can use:

- **Show Databases:**
```sql
SHOW DATABASES;
```

- **Create a Database:**
```sql
```

```sql
CREATE DATABASE dbname;
```

- **Use a Database:**
```sql
USE dbname;
```

- **Create a Table:**
```sql
CREATE TABLE tablename (
    id INT AUTO_INCREMENT PRIMARY KEY,
    name VARCHAR(100),
    age INT
);
```

- **Insert Data:**
```sql
INSERT INTO tablename (name, age)
VALUES ('John Doe', 30);
```

- **Query Data:**
```sql
SELECT * FROM tablename;
```

```
```

- **Delete Data:**
```sql
DELETE FROM tablename WHERE id = 1;
```

Understanding MySQL Workbench

MySQL Workbench is a graphical tool that simplifies database administration and offers powerful features for managing MySQL databases. It provides an intuitive interface for executing queries, designing databases, and managing server configurations. Here are some key features of MySQL Workbench:

- **Visual Database Design:** Create and manage database schemas through an easy-to-use graphical interface.
- **SQL Development:** Execute SQL queries with syntax highlighting and code intelligence.
- **Data Modeling:** Use the modeling tool to design complex databases and generate SQL scripts.
- **Server Administration:** Monitor server

status, manage user accounts, and configure server settings with ease.
- **Backup and Restore:** Perform backup and restoration of databases and tables.

Conclusion

MySQL is a robust and versatile database management system that plays a crucial role in a plethora of application environments. From its straightforward installation process to its powerful architecture, MySQL empowers users to efficiently store, manage, and query large datasets. Familiarity with its command-line interface and tools like MySQL Workbench allows developers and database administrators to maximize the benefits of MySQL, ensuring they can handle data effectively.

As you continue your journey with MySQL, remember that practice is key. Experiment with different commands, explore the documentation, and dive deeper into SQL to unlock the full potential of this powerful database system. Whether you are developing small applications or managing enterprise-level databases, MySQL provides the necessary tools and flexibility to grow with your needs.

2. Getting Started with MySQL

MySQL is one of the most popular open-source relational database management systems (RDBMS) in the world. It is known for its reliability, flexibility, and ease of use, making it a preferred choice for small applications to large-scale enterprise systems. MySQL supports various platforms and can handle large volumes of data, which makes it suitable for a range of applications. This guide will help you get started with MySQL by covering essential aspects such as connecting to MySQL, using the MySQL Command Line Interface (CLI), and understanding MySQL Workbench.

Connecting to MySQL

Connecting to a MySQL database involves establishing a link between your application or command line interface and the MySQL server. Below is a step-by-step guide on how to connect to MySQL:

Step 1: Install MySQL Server

Before diving into connecting to MySQL, ensure that MySQL is installed on your system. You can download the installer from the [MySQL website] (https://dev.mysql.com/downloads/mysql/). Follow the installation instructions specific to your operating system (Windows, macOS, or Linux). The installation procedure usually involves setting the root password and configuring additional settings.

Step 2: Starting the MySQL Server

Once the installation process is complete, you must ensure that the MySQL server is running.

- **Windows:** Open the Command Prompt and run the command:
  ```cmd
  net start mysql
  ```

- **macOS/Linux:** You can start MySQL using the following command:
  ```bash
  ```

```
  sudo service mysqld start   # For some
distributions
  sudo systemctl start mysql   # For others
  ```
```

You might need administrator or superuser permissions to perform these commands.

### Step 3: Using MySQL Client to Connect

You can connect to the MySQL server using the MySQL client. To connect using the command line, open the terminal (or Command Prompt on Windows) and execute the following command:

```bash
mysql -u root -p
```

- `-u root` indicates you're connecting as the root user (the default administrative user).
- `-p` prompts you for your password. After entering the password you set up during installation, you will enter the MySQL command-line environment.
```

Step 4: Establishing Connections from Applications

If you're connecting to MySQL from an application (for example, a web app using PHP or Node.js), you'll usually set up your connection string with parameters like the hostname, username, password, and database name. Here's an example of connecting using the MySQLi extension in PHP:

```php
$servername = "localhost";
$username = "root";
$password = "your_password";
$dbname = "your_database";

$conn = new mysqli($servername, $username, $password, $dbname);

// Check connection
if ($conn->connect_error) {
    die("Connection failed: " . $conn->connect_error);
}
echo "Connected successfully";
```

Step 5: Access Database

Once connected, you can perform various operations such as creating databases, tables, and running queries.

MySQL Command Line Interface

The MySQL Command Line Interface (CLI) is one of the primary means of interacting with MySQL servers. It provides a powerful and flexible way to manage databases and execute SQL queries.

Basic Commands in MySQL CLI

1. **Show Databases**
   ```sql
   SHOW DATABASES;
   ```
   This command lists all databases on the MySQL server.

2. **Creating a Database**
   ```sql
   CREATE DATABASE my_database;
   ```

```
```

This command creates a new database named `my_database`.

3. **Use a Database**
```sql
USE my_database;
```

Selecting a database for subsequent operations.

4. **Creating a Table**
```sql
CREATE TABLE users (
    id INT AUTO_INCREMENT PRIMARY KEY,
    username VARCHAR(50) NOT NULL,
    password VARCHAR(255) NOT NULL
);
```

This command creates a `users` table with three columns.

5. **Inserting Data**
```sql
INSERT INTO users (username, password)
VALUES ('john_doe', 'secure_pass');
```

```
```

This statement adds a new record to the `users` table.

6. **Querying Data**
   ```sql
   SELECT * FROM users;
   ```

   Fetches all records from the `users` table.

7. **Updating Data**
   ```sql
   UPDATE users SET password =
   'new_secure_pass' WHERE username =
   'john_doe';
   ```

   Modifies an existing record.

8. **Deleting Data**
   ```sql
   DELETE FROM users WHERE username =
   'john_doe';
   ```

   Deletes a record from the table.

Command-Line Shortcuts and Tips

- **Exiting the CLI:** Type `exit` or `quit` to leave the MySQL command line.
- **Help Command:** Use `HELP;` or `\h` to see available commands.
- **Auto-Completion:** Use the Tab key to auto-complete commands and table names.
- **SQL File Execution:** If you have SQL commands saved in a file (e.g., `commands.sql`), you can execute them using:
```sql
SOURCE /path/to/commands.sql;
```

Error Handling

While operating from the CLI, you may encounter various errors. Here are some common ones:

- **Access Denied:** If you see an "Access denied" error, ensure your user has the appropriate privileges or check the username/password.
- **Unknown Database:** This occurs if you try to use or query a database that does not exist.
- **Syntax Errors:** Recheck your SQL

syntax as it is vital to be accurate when entering commands.

Understanding MySQL Workbench

MySQL Workbench is a graphical user interface (GUI) that allows for easier management of MySQL databases. It provides tools for database design, SQL development, server administration, and maintenance.

Features of MySQL Workbench

1. **Database Design:** Allows you to create and modify database structures visually using a drag-and-drop interface.

2. **SQL Editor:** Provides an integrated environment to write, execute, and manage SQL queries. This includes syntax highlighting and auto-completion features.

3. **Database Administration:** You can manage users, configure server settings, monitor performance, and handle backups and restore procedures.

4. **Data Modeling:** Helps create Entity-Relationship Diagrams (ERDs) to visually depict relationships between tables.

5. **Migration:** You can migrate from other databases like Microsoft SQL Server or Oracle Database using the built-in Migration Wizard.

Getting Started with MySQL Workbench

1. **Download and Install:**
   Download MySQL Workbench from the [official website] (https://dev.mysql.com/downloads/workbench/). Follow the installation process.

2. **Connecting to MySQL:**
   - Open MySQL Workbench.
   - Click on `Database` > `Connect to Database` or click on the `+` icon next to `MySQL Connections`.
   - Enter the connection details including hostname (usually `localhost`), the username, and password.

3. **Navigating the Interface:**

- **Navigator Panel:** Displays existing connections, schemas, tables, and other database objects.
- **SQL Editor:** Where you can write and execute SQL queries.
- **Output Panel:** Shows results of executed queries and any error messages.

Executing SQL Queries in Workbench

1. **Query Execution:** Type your query into the SQL editor, and click the lightning bolt icon (Execute) or press `Ctrl + Enter` (Windows) / `Command + Enter` (macOS) to run it.

2. **Saving Queries:** You can save your SQL scripts for future use by choosing `File` > `Save Script`.

3. **Results Display:** Query results will show up in a separate results grid beneath the SQL editor, making it easy to view and analyze results.

Visual Tools for Database Management

1. **Data Modeling:** Create new models using the `File` > `New Model`. Define entities, attributes, and relationships visually.

2. **Synchronizing Models:** You can sync a model with an existing database to apply changes.

3. **Performance Monitoring:** Workbench includes a performance dashboard that provides insights into server health and performance metrics.

Exporting and Importing Data

MySQL Workbench allows easy data transfer. You can export data to formats like CSV, JSON, or SQL scripts. To import data, you can use the import wizard.

Backups and Restores

To back up your databases, use the 'Data Export' feature under `Server`. You can also restore a database using the 'Data Import' feature when needed.

Conclusion

Establishing a solid foundational understanding of MySQL, including connecting to MySQL, utilizing the MySQL Command Line Interface, and leveraging MySQL Workbench, is crucial for effective database management and manipulation. As you progress through more advanced topics such as optimization, indexing, and transactions, having these foundational skills will be indispensable. Each of these tools offers distinct advantages and workflows, so familiarize yourself with each to find the combination that works best for your specific use cases.

By mastering these tools and their functionalities, you'll be well-equipped to manage and harness the full power of MySQL, paving the way for building robust and scalable applications that rely on this versatile database system.

3.Database Design: A Comprehensive Guide

Database design is a fundamental aspect of software development that ensures data is stored efficiently, accurately, and securely. In this guide, we will delve deep into the essential components of database design, covering an understanding of databases and tables, data types in MySQL, and methods of normalization and database schema design.

Understanding Databases and Tables

What is a Database?

A database is an organized collection of structured information or data typically stored electronically in a computer system. Databases are managed by Database Management Systems (DBMS), which allow users to create, read, update, and delete data in the database. The main purpose of a database is to store large amounts of structured information and enable easy access to that information whenever needed.

Types of Databases

There are several types of databases, including:

1. **Relational Databases**: These databases store data in tables. Each table consists of rows and columns, and relationships can be established between different tables. Examples include MySQL, PostgreSQL, and Oracle.

2. **NoSQL Databases**: NoSQL databases do not use a fixed schema and are useful for storing unstructured data. They can be document-based (MongoDB), key-value stores (Redis), column-family stores (Cassandra), or graph databases (Neo4j).

3. **Distributed Databases**: These databases are spread across multiple locations, which might be on the same network or geographically dispersed.

4. **Cloud Databases**: Essentially a type of distributed database, cloud databases are hosted on cloud computing platforms allowing

flexible scalability and availability.

What is a Table?

In a relational database, data is structured into tables. A table consists of rows and columns, where:

- **Columns**: Each column represents a specific attribute, such as a person's name or a product price.

- **Rows**: Each row, also known as a record, represents a single entry or instance of that data, for example, details about a specific customer or a specific transaction.

Relationships Between Tables

Tables can be related to each other through various types of relationships:

1. **One-to-One**: Each row in Table A is linked to a unique row in Table B. An example would be a table of users and a table for user profiles.

2. **One-to-Many**: A single record in Table A can be linked to multiple records in Table B. For instance, one customer can have many orders.

3. **Many-to-Many**: Records in Table A can relate to multiple records in Table B and vice versa. This is often implemented through a junction table.

Data Types in MySQL

MySQL, a popular relational database management system, offers a variety of data types that can be used in table column definitions. Choosing the correct data type is crucial for ensuring efficient storage and data integrity.

Numeric Data Types

MySQL has several numeric data types categorized into:

1. **Integer Types**: These can store whole numbers. Variants include TINYINT, SMALLINT, MEDIUMINT, INT, and

BIGINT. The size of the integer determines the amount of storage space used and the range of values.

2. **Floating Point Types**: Used to store approximate numeric data. For instance, FLOAT and DOUBLE can store decimal values. DECIMAL is used for fixed-point numbers.

String Data Types

String data types in MySQL include:

1. **CHAR**: A fixed-length string that can hold up to 255 characters. Always occupies the specified length.

2. **VARCHAR**: A variable-length string that can hold up to 65,535 characters. Storage size is based on the actual length of the string stored.

3. **TEXT Types**: Includes TINYTEXT, TEXT, MEDIUMTEXT, and LONGTEXT, which can store large amounts of text.

4. **BLOB Types**: Similar to TEXT types but intended for storing binary data like images or multimedia files.

Date and Time Data Types

MySQL provides various data types for handling date and time:

1. **DATE**: Stores date values (YYYY-MM-DD).

2. **TIME**: Stores time values (HH:MM:SS).

3. **DATETIME**: Stores both date and time (YYYY-MM-DD HH:MM:SS).

4. **TIMESTAMP**: Stores timestamp values in seconds since the epoch.

5. **YEAR**: Stores years in a 2 or 4-digit format.

Choosing the Right Data Type

Selecting the appropriate data type is vital

since it impacts data storage, retrieval speed, and overall database performance. Factors to consider while choosing data types include data nature, value range, and intended use, among others.

Normalization and Database Schema Design

What is Normalization?

Normalization is a systematic approach of organizing database tables to minimize data redundancy and improve data integrity. This process involves dividing large tables into smaller, related tables and defining relationships between them. Normalization typically encompasses several levels or "normal forms," each addressing specific types of anomalies.

First Normal Form (1NF)

A relation is in 1NF if:

1. All attributes contain atomic values (no repeating groups or arrays).

2. Each attribute value in the table is unique.

Example: A customer order table should not contain multiple entries in a single cell.

Second Normal Form (2NF)

A relation is in 2NF if:

1. It is already in 1NF.
2. All non-key attributes are fully functionally dependent on the primary key.

Example: In a table of students and their courses, the course name should not be in the same table if it depends only on the course ID, not the student.

Third Normal Form (3NF)

A relation is in 3NF if:

1. It is in 2NF.
2. There are no transitive functional dependencies (non-key attributes do not depend on other non-key attributes).

Example: Customer addresses should be stored in a separate table if they are dependent only on customer ID.

Database Schema Design

Database schema refers to the blueprint of how data is organized in a database. It outlines the tables, fields, relationships, views, indexes, and other elements necessary for effective database function.

Sure! Below are explanations of the basic SQL statements along with examples for each.

1. SELECT Statement
The `SELECT` statement is used to retrieve data from one or more tables.

Example:
```sql
SELECT first_name, last_name
FROM employees
WHERE department = 'Sales';
```

*This query retrieves the first and last names

of employees who work in the Sales
department.*

2. INSERT Statement
The `INSERT` statement is used to add new
records to a table.

Example:
```sql
INSERT INTO employees (first_name,
last_name, department, hire_date)
VALUES ('John', 'Doe', 'Marketing', '2023-01-
15');
```

*This query adds a new employee named John
Doe in the Marketing department with a hire
date of January 15, 2023.*

3. UPDATE Statement
The `UPDATE` statement is used to modify
existing records in a table.

Example:
```sql
UPDATE employees
SET department = 'Human Resources'
WHERE last_name = 'Doe';
```

```

*This query changes the department of all employees with the last name "Doe" to Human Resources.*

### 4. DELETE Statement
The `DELETE` statement is used to remove records from a table.

**Example:**
```sql
DELETE FROM employees
WHERE last_name = 'Doe' AND first_name = 'John';
```

This query deletes the record of the employee named John Doe from the employees table.

These basic SQL statements form the foundation for interacting with databases.

Steps in Database Schema Design

1. **Requirement Analysis**: Gather requirements from stakeholders to understand
```

the data needs.

2. **Conceptual Design**: Create an Entity-Relationship (ER) model to visually represent entities and relationships.

3. **Logical Design**: Convert the ER model into a logical structure using normalization principles.

4. **Physical Design**: Specify how the data will be physically stored in the database, including performance considerations.

Best Practices for Schema Design

- **Use Meaningful Names**: Table and column names should convey the actual content and purpose clearly.

- **Avoid Redundancy**: Normalize the data to prevent duplicate data entries as much as possible.

- **Implement Foreign Keys**: Use foreign keys to enforce relationships and maintain referential integrity between tables.

- **Index Strategically**: Create indexes on columns frequently searched or used in joins to enhance query performance.

- **Document the Design**: Maintain thorough documentation of the schema and any relationships, which aids maintenance and future development.

Database design is a crucial step in software development that significantly impacts data integrity, performance, and scalability. Understanding the structure of databases and tables, the significance of appropriate data types, and the principles of normalization are key components to creating a robust database. Moreover, proper database schema design creates a strong foundation for any software application, facilitating efficient data retrieval and management while allowing for future growth and iterations. Mastery of these concepts is essential for anyone involved in database or software engineering.

4.Advanced SQL Queries in MySQL

Structured Query Language (SQL) is a powerful tool used for managing and manipulating relational databases. MySQL, one of the most popular database management systems, allows users to perform a variety of operations with SQL. This guide will cover some advanced SQL queries in MySQL, focusing on essential topics such as JOIN operations, subqueries, grouping and aggregating data, and using CASE statements. These concepts are vital for anyone looking to enhance their database querying skills.

JOIN Operations

JOIN operations are fundamental for combining rows from two or more tables based on related columns. They allow for efficient data retrieval from relational databases where data is often normalized across several tables. MySQL supports several types of JOIN operations:

1. INNER JOIN

An INNER JOIN returns records that have matching values in both tables involved in the join. It is the most common type of join.

Example:

```sql
SELECT a.employee_id, a.first_name,
a.last_name, b.department_name
FROM employees AS a
INNER JOIN departments AS b ON
a.department_id = b.department_id;
```

In this query, we select employee details along with their department names by joining the `employees` table (aliased as `a`) with the `departments` table (aliased as `b`).

2. LEFT JOIN

A LEFT JOIN returns all records from the left table and the matched records from the right table. If there is no match, NULL values will be returned for the right table's columns.

Example:

```sql
SELECT a.employee_id, a.first_name,
b.department_name
FROM employees AS a
LEFT JOIN departments AS b ON
a.department_id = b.department_id;
```

In this case, all employees will be listed, including those who may not be assigned to a department.

3. RIGHT JOIN

A RIGHT JOIN is similar to a LEFT JOIN, but it returns all records from the right table and matched records from the left table. If there is no match, NULL values will be returned for the left table's columns.

Example:

```sql
SELECT a.employee_id, a.first_name,
b.department_name
```

```
FROM employees AS a
RIGHT JOIN departments AS b ON
a.department_id = b.department_id;
```

This will list all departments, including those
that may not have any employees assigned.

4. FULL OUTER JOIN

MySQL does not directly support FULL
OUTER JOIN, but it can be mimicked using a
combination of LEFT JOIN and RIGHT JOIN
with a UNION.

Example:

```sql
SELECT a.employee_id, a.first_name,
b.department_name
FROM employees AS a
LEFT JOIN departments AS b ON
a.department_id = b.department_id

UNION

SELECT a.employee_id, a.first_name,
```

b.department_name
FROM employees AS a
RIGHT JOIN departments AS b ON
a.department_id = b.department_id;
```

In this query, we retrieve all employees and all departments, ensuring no data is lost from either side of the join.

### 5. CROSS JOIN

A CROSS JOIN produces a Cartesian product between two tables, meaning every row in the first table is combined with every row in the second table.

**Example:**

```sql
SELECT a.employee_id, a.first_name,
b.project_name
FROM employees AS a
CROSS JOIN projects AS b;
```

This will generate a combination of every
```

employee with every project.

6. Self JOIN

A self JOIN is a regular join but the table is joined with itself. This is useful for querying hierarchical data.

Example:

```sql
SELECT a.employee_id, a.first_name,
b.first_name AS manager_name
FROM employees AS a
INNER JOIN employees AS b ON
a.manager_id = b.employee_id;
```

This query retrieves employees alongside their managers' names by relating the `manager_id` to the `employee_id`.

Subqueries

Subqueries, or nested queries, allow you to use the result of one query as an input to another. They can be used in SELECT,

INSERT, UPDATE, and DELETE statements.

1. Subquery in SELECT

Subqueries can be embedded in the SELECT clause to compute values dynamically.

Example:

```sql
SELECT employee_id, first_name, last_name,
    (SELECT department_name FROM
departments WHERE department_id =
employees.department_id) AS
department_name
FROM employees;
```

This query includes a subquery that retrieves the department name for each employee.

2. Subquery in WHERE

Subqueries can be used in the WHERE clause to filter results.

Example:

```sql
SELECT employee_id, first_name, last_name
FROM employees
WHERE department_id IN (SELECT
department_id FROM departments WHERE
location_id = '1000');
```

In this case, we retrieve employees who are in
departments located in a specific location.

3. Correlated Subquery

A correlated subquery uses values from the
outer query in its execution.

Example:

```sql
SELECT a.employee_id, a.first_name
FROM employees AS a
WHERE a.salary > (SELECT AVG(salary)
FROM employees AS b WHERE
a.department_id = b.department_id);
```

This query retrieves employees who earn more than the average salary in their respective departments.

Grouping and Aggregating Data

Grouping and aggregating data with SQL is essential for summarizing and analyzing information. The `GROUP BY` clause groups rows sharing a property and allows for the use of aggregate functions like COUNT, SUM, AVG, MAX, and MIN.

1. GROUP BY Clause

The `GROUP BY` clause groups records with identical values in specified columns.

Example:

```sql
SELECT department_id, COUNT(*) AS number_of_employees
FROM employees
GROUP BY department_id;
```

This query returns the number of employees in each department.

2. Aggregate Functions

Aggregate functions consolidate the data over a group defined by the `GROUP BY` clause.

Example with SUM:

```sql
SELECT department_id, SUM(salary) AS total_salaries
FROM employees
GROUP BY department_id;
```

This retrieves the total salary of employees in each department.

3. HAVING Clause

The `HAVING` clause is used to filter records after the aggregation.

Example:

```sql
SELECT department_id, COUNT(*) AS
number_of_employees
FROM employees
GROUP BY department_id
HAVING COUNT(*) > 5;
```

This gets departments that have more than
five employees.

4. Using Multiple Aggregates

You can apply multiple aggregate functions in
a single query.

Example:

```sql
SELECT department_id, COUNT(*) AS
number_of_employees, AVG(salary) AS
average_salary
FROM employees
GROUP BY department_id;
```

This provides both the count of employees

and their average salary per department.

Using CASE Statements

CASE statements allow for conditional logic within SQL queries, enabling you to create complex results based on specific criteria.

1. Simple CASE Statements

A simple CASE statement compares an expression against a set of values.

Example:

```sql
SELECT employee_id, first_name, last_name,
    CASE department_id
        WHEN 1 THEN 'Sales'
        WHEN 2 THEN 'HR'
        WHEN 3 THEN 'IT'
        ELSE 'Other'
    END AS department_name
FROM employees;
```

Here, we use a simple CASE to label

departments based on their IDs.

2. Searched CASE Statements

Searched CASE statements allow for more complex conditions that can evaluate to true based on a condition.

Example:

```sql
SELECT employee_id, first_name, last_name, salary,
    CASE
        WHEN salary < 30000 THEN 'Low'
        WHEN salary BETWEEN 30000 AND 70000 THEN 'Medium'
        ELSE 'High'
    END AS salary_range
FROM employees;
```

This categorizes each employee's salary into low, medium, or high.

3. Using CASE within Aggregate Functions

You can also use CASE statements inside aggregate functions for conditional aggregation.

Example:

```sql
SELECT department_id,
    COUNT(CASE WHEN gender = 'M'
THEN 1 END) AS male_count,
    COUNT(CASE WHEN gender = 'F'
THEN 1 END) AS female_count
FROM employees
GROUP BY department_id;
```

This counts the number of male and female employees within each department.

Conclusion

Advanced SQL queries in MySQL are powerful tools for effective data analysis and manipulation. Mastering JOIN operations, subqueries, grouping and aggregating data, and the use of CASE statements can significantly enhance your ability to interact with and derive meaningful insights from your data. With practice, these complex queries will become second nature and empower you to tackle various database challenges.

By implementing the numerous examples illustrated in this guide, you can build a solid foundation for writing advanced SQL queries that serve real-world application needs in MySQL databases.

5.Indexing and Performance Optimization in MySQL

MySQL is one of the most popular relational database management systems (RDBMS) that allows users to manage data efficiently. As applications grow and the amount of data increases, the performance of the database can degrade if not properly optimized. Indexing is a key technique for improving the speed of data retrieval operations on a database table. This document will explore the concepts of indexing and performance optimization in MySQL, covering understanding indexes, creating and managing indexes, as well as query optimization techniques.

1. Understanding Indexes

An index in a database is similar to an index in a book. It allows the database management system to find rows in a table more efficiently without having to scan every row. Indexes are critical for optimizing the performance of SELECT queries, as they help to quickly locate data without scanning the entire table.

1.1 Types of Indexes

1. **Primary Index**: This is automatically created for the primary key of the table. It ensures that the values are unique and not NULL. When a primary key is defined, MySQL creates a clustered index.

2. **Unique Index**: A unique index ensures that all values in a column (or a group of columns) are distinct. Unlike primary keys, unique indexes can accept NULL values unless specified otherwise.

3. **Non-Unique Index**: This type of index does not enforce uniqueness. It is used merely for performance purposes to speed up query performance.

4. **Full-Text Index**: This index allows for natural language searches on text-based columns. It's optimized for scenarios where full-text searches are needed, such as searching for keywords within a large body of text.

5. **Spatial Index**: Used for spatial data

types, this index is specifically designed for optimizing spatial queries and searches.

1.2 How Indexes Work

When a query is executed that includes a WHERE clause, MySQL uses indexes to find which rows satisfy the condition without having to perform a full table scan. The table data is organized in a way that can significantly reduce the number of disk I/O operations required to retrieve the data.

MySQL uses different types of data structures to implement indexes:

- **B-Trees**: The most common structure, used for most types of indexes.
- **Hashes**: Used primarily for memory tables and exact match lookup.
- **Inverted Index**: Utilized for full-text searches.

1.3 Costs of Using Indexes

While indexes significantly speed up read operations, they come with costs. Each index consumes additional disk space and can slow down write operations such as INSERT, UPDATE, and DELETE, because the indexes need to be updated whenever data is modified. It's crucial to strike a balance when determining which indexes to implement.

2. Creating and Managing Indexes

2.1 Creating Indexes

In MySQL, indexes can be created using the `CREATE INDEX` statement. The syntax of creating an index is:

```sql
CREATE INDEX index_name ON
table_name (column1, column2, ...);
```

Example: Creating a Basic Index

Let's say we have a table called `users`, and we want to speed up queries that search based on the `last_name` column:

```sql
```

CREATE INDEX idx_last_name ON users (last_name);
```

We can also create a unique index:

```sql
CREATE UNIQUE INDEX idx_email ON users (email);
```

Example: Creating a Composite Index

When queries filter based on multiple columns, a composite index might be beneficial.

```sql
CREATE INDEX idx_name_age ON users (last_name, age);
```

In this case, the index would be used to optimize queries that filter based on both `last_name` and `age` together.
```

2.2 Managing Indexes

Once created, indexes can be managed using various commands. Some common operations include:

- **View existing indexes**:

```sql
SHOW INDEX FROM table_name;
```

- **Drop an index**:

```sql
DROP INDEX index_name ON table_name;
```

2.3 Altering a Table for Indexes

You can also add indexes when creating a table using the `CREATE TABLE` statement:

```sql
CREATE TABLE users (
    id INT AUTO_INCREMENT PRIMARY KEY,
```

```
    first_name VARCHAR(50),
    last_name VARCHAR(50),
    email VARCHAR(100) UNIQUE,
    age INT,
    INDEX idx_last_name (last_name),
    INDEX idx_name_age (last_name, age)
);
```

3. Query Optimization Techniques

3.1 Analyzing Queries

To optimize the performance of your queries, start by analyzing the execution plans using the `EXPLAIN` statement. This command gives insights into how MySQL executes a query and whether indexes are being used effectively.

```sql
EXPLAIN SELECT * FROM users WHERE last_name = 'Smith';
```

The output will show whether MySQL is utilizing any indexes and how many rows it estimates will be scanned.

3.2 Use of Query Cache

MySQL has a query cache that can store the results of SELECT statements, allowing subsequent identical queries to return results without executing the statement again. However, effective use of this feature can vary, depending on whether your data changes frequently. You can enable it in the MySQL configuration:

```sql
SET GLOBAL query_cache_size = 1048576; -- 1MB
SET GLOBAL query_cache_type = 1;  -- Enable caching
```

3.3 Normalization and Denormalization

Normalization reduces data redundancy by structuring the database into smaller tables and defining relationships between them. This can lead to complex queries that may necessitate JOIN operations, which can be slowing.

In some specific scenarios where performance is more critical than data integrity or redundancy, denormalization (adding redundant data) might improve performance by reducing the number of JOINs needed in queries.

3.4 Limit the Result Set

Whenever possible, limit the number of rows returned by your queries using the `LIMIT` clause, especially when dealing with large datasets.

```sql
SELECT * FROM users WHERE last_name = 'Smith' LIMIT 10;
```

3.5 Use Proper Data Types

Choosing the correct data types for your fields can also enhance performance. For example, using `INT` for numeric values instead of `BIGINT` when not necessary will save space and can speed up operations. Smaller data types take less disk space and memory, enhancing overall performance during data retrieval.

3.6 Utilize Covering Indexes

A covering index is an index that contains all the columns required to satisfy a query. For example, if a SELECT statement requests columns `last_name` and `age`, and you have an index on both of these columns, the query can be satisfied using the index without having to touch the actual table.

```sql
CREATE INDEX idx_covering ON users (last_name, age);
```

3.7 Optimize JOIN Operations

When performing JOINs, ensure that you are joining on indexed columns. Also, consider the order of tables in your JOINs, as it can impact the performance. Smaller tables should generally be on the left side of the JOIN.

3.8 Use UNION All Instead of UNION

When combining results, if you're sure the records do not overlap, prefer `UNION ALL` to `UNION`. `UNION` performs a distinct operation which can significantly slow down execution time compared to `UNION ALL`, which simply concatenates results.

```sql
SELECT name FROM users WHERE age > 30
UNION ALL
SELECT name FROM users WHERE age <= 30;
```

3.9 Tune MySQL Configuration

MySQL has several configuration parameters that can impact performance. Common settings include:

- **innodb_buffer_pool_size**: This sets the amount of memory allocated for caching InnoDB data and indexes.
- **max_connections**: This setting controls

the maximum number of simultaneous client connections.
- **key_buffer_size**: This is for MyISAM tables and determines the memory allocated for indexing operations.

You can adjust these settings in the MySQL configuration file (`my.cnf` or `my.ini`).

3.10 Monitor Performance

Regularly monitor your MySQL server performance using tools like `SHOW STATUS`, `SHOW VARIABLES`, and performance statistics from the MySQL Performance Schema. This allows you to understand whether your indexes and optimizations are effective or whether further adjustments are necessary.

```sql
SHOW GLOBAL STATUS LIKE 'Handler %';
```

Monitoring helps identify slow queries, frequently accessed tables, and other performance insights that guide your optimization efforts.

Indexing and performance optimization are critical components of managing a MySQL database effectively. Understanding how indexes work, creating and managing them efficiently, and utilizing various query optimization techniques can lead to significant performance improvements. Careful analysis, monitoring, and tuning are essential to maintain an optimal database performance as application demands evolve. Following best practices in indexing and query design will ensure that your MySQL database remains responsive and efficient, even as data volumes grow. Always remember: while indexes boost read operations, they come with write overheads. Therefore, every index must be created with careful analysis of the application's specific querying patterns and workload demands.

6.Data Integrity and Constraints in MySQL

Data integrity is a fundamental aspect of database management systems (DBMS), ensuring the accuracy, consistency, and reliability of data stored in a database. MySQL, being one of the most popular relational database management systems, provides multiple levels of constraints to help maintain data integrity. This discussion will cover key concepts such as Primary and Foreign Keys, UNIQUE and CHECK constraints, as well as Transactions and ACID properties, all of which play a crucial role in maintaining data integrity while working with MySQL.

Primary Keys

A Primary Key is a specific choice of a minimal set of attributes (columns) in a database table that uniquely identifies a record within that table. A Primary Key must contain unique values, and it cannot contain NULL values. Here's how Primary Keys function and how to implement them:

Characteristics of Primary Keys

1. **Uniqueness:** Each value in a primary key must be unique across the table.
2. **Non-nullability:** A primary key cannot consist of NULL values.
3. **Immutability:** The values in a primary key should rarely change. If the primary key value is modified, it may affect referential integrity and relationships with other tables.

Example

Consider a simple table named `Employees`:

```sql
CREATE TABLE Employees (
    EmployeeID INT AUTO_INCREMENT,
    FirstName VARCHAR(50),
    LastName VARCHAR(50),
    PRIMARY KEY (EmployeeID)
);
```

In this example, `EmployeeID` serves as the

Primary Key. Each employee will have a unique `EmployeeID`, ensuring that no two employees can have the same identifier.

Foreign Keys

A Foreign Key is an attribute or a set of attributes in one table that references a Primary Key in another table. Foreign Keys are vital in establishing relationships between tables and enforcing referential integrity.

Characteristics of Foreign Keys

1. **Referential Integrity:** Foreign Keys ensure that a record in one table corresponds to a record in another table, preventing orphan records.
2. **Cascade Actions:** Foreign Keys can define cascade actions that affect related tables, such as cascading deletes or updates.

Example

Continuing with our `Employees` table, let's create a `Departments` table and establish a Foreign Key relationship:

```sql
CREATE TABLE Departments (
    DepartmentID INT AUTO_INCREMENT,
    DepartmentName VARCHAR(100),
    PRIMARY KEY (DepartmentID)
);

CREATE TABLE Employees (
    EmployeeID INT AUTO_INCREMENT,
    FirstName VARCHAR(50),
    LastName VARCHAR(50),
    DepartmentID INT,
    PRIMARY KEY (EmployeeID),
    FOREIGN KEY (DepartmentID)
REFERENCES Departments(DepartmentID)
ON DELETE CASCADE
);
```

In this example, `DepartmentID` in the `Employees` table acts as a Foreign Key that references the `DepartmentID` in the `Departments` table. The `ON DELETE CASCADE` clause ensures that if a department is deleted, all employees associated with that department are also deleted automatically, thus maintaining referential integrity.

UNIQUE and CHECK Constraints

UNIQUE Constraints

The UNIQUE constraint ensures that all values in a column are different from each other. Unlike the Primary Key, a table can have multiple UNIQUE constraints, and these can include NULL values (as long as all non-null values remain unique).

Example

```sql
CREATE TABLE Users (
    UserID INT AUTO_INCREMENT,
    Email VARCHAR(100) UNIQUE,
    Username VARCHAR(50) UNIQUE,
    Password VARCHAR(50),
    PRIMARY KEY (UserID)
);
```

In this `Users` table, both `Email` and

`Username` fields are enforced to contain unique values across all records, preventing duplicates.

CHECK Constraints

The CHECK constraint is used to ensure that all values in a column satisfy a specific condition. This is useful for data validation.

Example

```sql
CREATE TABLE Products (
    ProductID INT AUTO_INCREMENT,
    ProductName VARCHAR(100),
    Price DECIMAL(10, 2),
    Stock INT,
    CHECK (Price >= 0),
    CHECK (Stock >= 0),
    PRIMARY KEY (ProductID)
);
```

In the `Products` table, two CHECK constraints enforce that `Price` and `Stock` cannot have negative values. If an attempt is made to insert a product with a negative price or stock level, the database will reject that transaction.

Transactions and ACID Properties

Transactions are crucial for ensuring reliable data operations in a database. A transaction is a sequence of one or more SQL operations that are executed as a single unit of work. Transactions provide a way to group multiple operations so they can either all succeed or all fail, ensuring data integrity.

ACID Properties

ACID stands for Atomicity, Consistency, Isolation, and Durability—four properties that guarantee that database transactions are processed reliably.

1. **Atomicity:** This property ensures that all operations within a transaction are completed successfully; if any of the operations fail, the entire transaction fails, and the database state remains unchanged.

Example:
```sql
START TRANSACTION;
INSERT INTO Accounts (AccountID, Balance) VALUES (1, 100);
INSERT INTO Accounts (AccountID, Balance) VALUES (2, 200);
COMMIT; -- All inserts will be saved only if no errors occur
```

2. **Consistency:** This refers to the property that the database must always be in a valid state before and after a transaction. Any transaction must leave the database in a consistent state, meaning it adheres to all defined constraints, relational integrity rules, and triggers.

Example:
```sql
START TRANSACTION;
UPDATE Users SET Balance = Balance - 50 WHERE UserID = 1;
UPDATE Users SET Balance = Balance + 50 WHERE UserID = 2;
COMMIT;
```

```
```

In this example, the transaction maintains the consistent state of user balances.

3. **Isolation:** This property ensures that concurrent transactions do not affect each other. Each transaction should appear to execute in isolation from others. MySQL supports different transaction isolation levels, which can be adjusted as needed.

Example:
```sql
SET TRANSACTION ISOLATION
LEVEL SERIALIZABLE;
START TRANSACTION;
-- perform operations
COMMIT;
```

4. **Durability:** This property guarantees that once a transaction has been committed, it will remain so even in the event of a system crash or failure. MySQL uses transaction logs and other mechanisms to ensure durability.

Example:
```sql
START TRANSACTION;
INSERT INTO Items (ItemID, Quantity)
VALUES (1, 10);
COMMIT; -- This modification would
remain even after a crash.
```

Conclusion

Data integrity is paramount in MySQL and other relational databases. By using primary and foreign keys to enforce uniqueness and relationships, and applying constraints like UNIQUE and CHECK to validate data, database administrators can create robust data structures. Additionally, understanding and managing transactions through the ACID properties helps ensure that these data structures remain accurate and reliable, even under concurrent access and system failures.

These techniques not only improve the quality of the data but also enhance the overall integrity of the database, forming a strong foundation for any application that relies on accurate and consistent data. By mastering data integrity and constraints, developers and database administrators can build efficient, reliable systems that provide valuable insights and support real-world applications.

7. Stored Procedures and Functions in MySQL

In relational database management systems, particularly in MySQL, stored procedures and functions are essential components that help in encapsulating logic. They allow developers to write reusable code that can be executed on the database server itself. This ensures that complex operations or business logic are handled efficiently, minimizing the amount of data transferred between the application layer and the database server. Additionally, triggers automatically execute in response to specific events on a table, like inserts, updates, or deletes, which can help maintain the integrity of the data.

In this detailed guide, we will explore the creation of stored procedures, the usage of functions, and the implementation of triggers in MySQL, complete with examples.

1: Creating Stored Procedures

A stored procedure is a precompiled collection of one or more SQL statements that can be executed on demand. It can accept input parameters, perform operations such as modifying data, and return output results.

1.1 Syntax of Stored Procedures

The basic syntax for creating a stored procedure in MySQL can be summarized as follows:

```sql
CREATE PROCEDURE procedure_name
(parameters)
BEGIN
    -- SQL statements
END;
```

Parameters can be defined as `IN`, `OUT`, or `INOUT`:
- `IN`: specifies input parameters.
- `OUT`: specifies output parameters.
- `INOUT`: specifies parameters that can serve both as input and output.

1.2 Example: Creating a Simple Stored Procedure

Let's create a stored procedure that inserts a new employee into an `employees` table.

1. **Define the Table**:
```sql
CREATE TABLE employees (
   id INT AUTO_INCREMENT PRIMARY KEY,
   name VARCHAR(100),
   job_title VARCHAR(100),
   salary DECIMAL(10, 2)
);
```

2. **Create the Stored Procedure**:
```sql
DELIMITER //

CREATE PROCEDURE AddEmployee (
   IN emp_name VARCHAR(100),
   IN emp_job_title VARCHAR(100),
   IN emp_salary DECIMAL(10, 2)
)
BEGIN
```

```sql
    INSERT INTO employees (name, job_title, salary)
    VALUES (emp_name, emp_job_title, emp_salary);
END //

DELIMITER ;
```

3. **Call the Stored Procedure**:
```sql
CALL AddEmployee('John Doe', 'Software Engineer', 60000.00);
```

After executing the above command, a new entry for John Doe will be added to the `employees` table.

1.3 Example: Stored Procedure with Output

You can also define a stored procedure with an output parameter:

```sql
DELIMITER //
```

```sql
CREATE PROCEDURE GetEmployeeSalary
(
    IN emp_id INT,
    OUT emp_salary DECIMAL(10, 2)
)
BEGIN
    SELECT salary INTO emp_salary
    FROM employees
    WHERE id = emp_id;
END //

DELIMITER ;
```

You can call this procedure and retrieve the salary of an employee as follows:

```sql
SET @salary = 0;
CALL GetEmployeeSalary(1, @salary);
SELECT @salary; -- This will return the
salary of the employee with ID 1
```

Chapter 2: Using Functions

Functions in MySQL are similar to stored procedures, but they return a single value and can be used in SQL expressions.

2.1 Syntax of Functions

The basic syntax for creating a function is:

```sql
CREATE FUNCTION function_name
(parameters)
RETURNS return_data_type
BEGIN
    -- SQL statements
    RETURN value;
END;
```

2.2 Example: Creating a Simple Function

Let's create a function that retrieves the salary of an employee based on their ID.

1. **Create the Function**:
```sql
DELIMITER //
```

```sql
CREATE FUNCTION GetSalary(emp_id
INT)
RETURNS DECIMAL(10, 2)
BEGIN
    DECLARE emp_salary DECIMAL(10, 2);

    SELECT salary INTO emp_salary
    FROM employees
    WHERE id = emp_id;

    RETURN emp_salary;
END //

DELIMITER ;
```

2. **Using the Function**:
You can directly use this function in a SQL query:

```sql
SELECT GetSalary(1) AS Salary;
-- This will return the salary of the employee with ID 1
```

Chapter 3: Triggers in MySQL

Triggers are special types of stored programs that are automatically executed (or "triggered") in response to certain events on a specified table or view.

3.1 Types of Triggers

1. **BEFORE INSERT**: Triggered before an insert operation on a table.
2. **AFTER INSERT**: Triggered after an insert operation on a table.
3. **BEFORE UPDATE**: Triggered before an update operation on a table.
4. **AFTER UPDATE**: Triggered after an update operation on a table.
5. **BEFORE DELETE**: Triggered before a delete operation on a table.
6. **AFTER DELETE**: Triggered after a delete operation on a table.

3.2 Syntax of Triggers

The basic syntax for creating a trigger is:

```sql
```

```
CREATE TRIGGER trigger_name
BEFORE|AFTER INSERT|UPDATE|
DELETE
ON table_name
FOR EACH ROW
BEGIN
    -- Trigger logic
END;
```

3.3 Example: Creating a Trigger

Let's create a trigger that will automatically log any insert operations to an `audit_log` table.

1. **Define the Audit Table**:
```sql
CREATE TABLE audit_log (
    id INT AUTO_INCREMENT PRIMARY KEY,
    employee_id INT,
    action VARCHAR(50),
    action_time TIMESTAMP DEFAULT CURRENT_TIMESTAMP
);
```

2. **Create the Trigger**:
```sql
DELIMITER //

CREATE TRIGGER AfterEmployeeInsert
AFTER INSERT ON employees
FOR EACH ROW
BEGIN
    INSERT INTO audit_log (employee_id, action)
    VALUES (NEW.id, 'Inserted');
END //

DELIMITER ;
```

In this case, every time a new employee is inserted into the `employees` table, a corresponding record is created in the `audit_log` table.

3. **Test the Trigger**:
First, insert a new employee:

```sql
CALL AddEmployee('Jane Doe', 'Project
```

Manager', 85000.00);
```

Then, check the `audit_log` table:

```sql
SELECT * FROM audit_log;
```

You should see a new entry indicating that an employee was inserted.

Conclusion

Stored procedures, functions, and triggers are powerful tools in MySQL that allow for the encapsulation of complex logic directly in the database layer. By utilizing these features, developers can create maintainable, scalable applications with efficient data manipulation capabilities. Stored procedures maximize performance by reducing network traffic and encapsulating business logic, while functions provide rapid access to calculated values. Triggers automate responses to data changes, ensuring consistency and integrity without manual intervention. These tools enrich the
```

functionality of MySQL and are essential for any database professional.

By understanding and implementing stored procedures, functions, and triggers, developers can significantly improve their database applications, making them more robust and efficient. Whether you're performing complex transactions, calculating derived values, or automatically maintaining logs, these features are fundamental components of any serious database application development in MySQL.

8. User Management and Security in MySQL

User management and security are critical components for any relational database management system (RDBMS), particularly with MySQL, which is widely used for web applications, corporate databases, and even big data applications due to its flexibility, robustness, and ease of use. Managing users effectively ensures that only authorized personnel have access to sensitive data, while security best practices can prevent unauthorized access, data leaks, and potential breaches.

Creating and Managing Users

MySQL provides a sophisticated user management system that allows administrators to create, modify, and delete user accounts. User accounts are identified by a unique username and host.

Creating Users

To create a new user in MySQL, you can use the `CREATE USER` statement. Here's an example of how to create a user:

```sql
CREATE USER 'newuser'@'localhost' IDENTIFIED BY 'password123';
```

In this example:
- `'newuser'` is the username.
- `@'localhost'` means that this user can only connect to the MySQL server from the local machine.
- `IDENTIFIED BY 'password123'` sets the password for the user.

Managing Users

Once a user is created, it can be modified as needed. Here are some of the common operations related to user management:

1. **Changing a Password**: You can change a user's password using the `ALTER USER` command:

```sql
ALTER USER 'newuser'@'localhost'
IDENTIFIED BY 'newpassword456';
```

2. **Renaming a User**: To rename a user,
you can use the `RENAME USER` command:

```sql
RENAME USER 'newuser'@'localhost' TO
'renameduser'@'localhost';
```

3. **Deleting a User**: If a user is no longer
needed, you can delete them:

```sql
DROP USER 'renameduser'@'localhost';
```

4. **Listing Users**: If you want to see all
the users created in your MySQL database,
you can query the `mysql.user` table:

```sql
SELECT User, Host FROM mysql.user;
```

```

```

User Authentication

MySQL supports several authentication plugins, which can enhance security. For example, you can enforce password complexity and expiration rules using plugins like `caching_sha2_password` or `mysql_native_password`. You can specify the authentication plugin when creating a user:

```sql
CREATE USER 'secureuser'@'localhost'
IDENTIFIED WITH
'caching_sha2_password' BY
'StrongPassword!';
```

Granting and Revoking Privileges

In MySQL, users can be granted specific privileges that determine their access levels. Privileges can be as simple as allowing a user to connect to the database, or as complex as enabling data modification and schema management.

Granting Privileges

To grant privileges to a user, you will use the `GRANT` statement. Here's an example of how to grant various privileges:

```sql
GRANT SELECT, INSERT, UPDATE ON mydatabase.* TO 'newuser'@'localhost';
```

In this command:
- `SELECT`, `INSERT`, and `UPDATE` are the privileges being granted.
- `mydatabase.*` signifies that these privileges apply to all tables in `mydatabase`.
- `'newuser'@'localhost'` is the user that will receive these privileges.

You can also grant all privileges on a database to a user:

```sql
GRANT ALL PRIVILEGES ON mydatabase.* TO 'newuser'@'localhost';
```

After granting privileges, it's essential to run the `FLUSH PRIVILEGES;` command to ensure that MySQL reloads the privileges immediately.

Revoking Privileges

If you find that a user no longer requires certain privileges, you can revoke them using the `REVOKE` statement:

```sql
REVOKE INSERT ON mydatabase.* FROM 'newuser'@'localhost';
```

This command will revoke the `INSERT` privilege from `newuser` for all tables in `mydatabase`.

You may also revoke all privileges granted to a user using:

```sql
REVOKE ALL PRIVILEGES ON mydatabase.* FROM 'newuser'@'localhost';
```

Checking Privileges

To see what privileges a user has, use the `SHOW GRANTS` command:

```sql
SHOW GRANTS FOR 'newuser'@'localhost';
```

This command will return a list of all the grants that apply to the specified user.

MySQL Security Best Practices

Implementing solid security practices is essential in safeguarding a MySQL database against unauthorized access and attacks. Here are some of the best practices for MySQL security:

1. Use Strong Passwords

Always enforce strong password policies. Passwords should be at least 12 characters long, incorporating upper and lower case letters, numbers, and special characters. You can set MySQL to enforce password validation:

```sql
SET GLOBAL validate_password_policy=2;
```

This will enforce a strong password policy where users must create complex passwords.

2. Use Least Privilege Principle

Always grant the minimum privileges necessary for users to perform their job functions. Avoid using the `GRANT ALL PRIVILEGES` command without specific justification.

3. Regularly Update MySQL

Keep MySQL updated to the latest version. Security vulnerabilities are regularly discovered and fixed, and running the latest version will help protect your database from known exploits.

4. Use SSL Connections

Enforce SSL/TLS for client connections to encrypt data in transit. In your MySQL configuration, you can require SSL connections by setting:

```ini
[mysqld]
require_secure_transport = ON
```

5. Limit User Connections

Limit the number of connections a user can create to prevent denial of service. You can do this during user creation:

```sql
CREATE USER 'limiteduser'@'localhost'
WITH MAX_CONNECTIONS 5;
```

6. Regular Backups

Perform regular backups of your MySQL databases. Use both logical backup methods like `mysqldump` and physical methods. Store backups in a secure location and test them frequently to ensure they can be restored when needed.

7. Monitor and Auditing

Keep an audit log of all changes and access events. Use MySQL's general log and slow query log for monitoring. Consider implementing third-party logging and monitoring solutions that can alert you to unusual patterns of access.

8. Firewall Configuration

Place your MySQL server behind a firewall and configure the firewall rules to allow connections only from trusted IP addresses. This can significantly reduce unauthorized access attempts.

9. Review and Revise User Accounts Regularly

Perform regular reviews of user accounts and their associated privileges. Remove any accounts that are no longer needed and adjust privileges as necessary.

User management and security are fundamental to maintaining the integrity and security of a MySQL database. By effectively creating and managing users, granting and revoking privileges, and following MySQL security best practices, organizations can safeguard sensitive information, manage access effectively, and maintain a secure database environment. The effort put into rigorous user management and robust security practices will pay dividends in protecting your organization's data assets.

9.Backup and Recovery in MySQL

Data is the lifeblood of modern applications and businesses. Given the critical importance of data, creating a robust backup and recovery strategy is essential to protect against data loss due to hardware failures, corruption, human error, or other unforeseen incidents. In this comprehensive guide, we will explore various backup strategies in MySQL, the use of the `mysqldump` utility for creating backups, and the processes involved in restoring databases effectively.

Backup Strategies

When devising a backup strategy for MySQL databases, there are several approaches that can be considered, depending on factors such as the size of the database, the importance of the data, and the frequency of changes. Below are some common backup strategies:

1. Full Backups

A full backup is an exact copy of the entire

database. This type of backup captures all the data, schema, and other necessary database components. Full backups are essential for new databases or periodic snapshots to ensure a baseline state that can be easily restored.

Pros
- Simple to implement and restore.
- Provides a complete snapshot usable for point-in-time recovery.

Cons
- Time-consuming and resource-intensive, especially for large databases.
- Requires significant storage space.

2. Incremental Backups

Incremental backups capture only the changes made since the last backup (either a full or incremental backup). This strategy is much more efficient in terms of storage and time but requires more complex recovery procedures.

Pros
- Faster and smaller than full backups.
- Conserves storage space.

Cons
- More complex to manage.
- A full restore requires the last full backup and all subsequent incremental backups.

3. Differential Backups

Differential backups capture all changes made since the last full backup. This means that each differential backup can grow in size until the next full backup is created.

Pros
- Easier to manage than incremental backups.
- Requires fewer backup files for a restore than incremental backups.

Cons
- Can consume more storage than incremental backups over time.
- Not as efficient as incremental backups for long periods without a full backup.

4. Binary Log Backups

MySQL maintains binary logs, which record

all changes to the database (DML statements) alongside the schema changes (DDL statements). These logs can be used to replay changes after restoring a backup, providing a more granular recovery option.

Pros
- Enables point-in-time recovery by capturing every change made since the last backup.
- Works well with a combination of full and incremental backups.

Cons
- Requires additional management of binlogs.
- Needs to be configured and purged regularly to avoid excessive storage usage.

Choosing the Right Strategy

The right backup strategy depends on the size of your database, your recovery time objectives (RTO), recovery point objectives (RPO), and the nature of your application. For instance, a high-traffic e-commerce site might opt for a combination of full weekly backups, daily incremental backups, and continuous binary logging for minimal data loss.

Using mysqldump

`mysqldump` is a command-line utility for creating logical backups of MySQL databases. It generates a set of SQL statements that can be used to reconstruct the database, which makes it ideal for smaller databases or situations where portability is desired.

Basic Syntax

The basic syntax of the `mysqldump` command is:

```bash
mysqldump [options] database_name > backup_file.sql
```

Example: Creating a Full Backup

To perform a full backup of a database named `mydatabase`, the command would be:

```bash
mysqldump -u username -p mydatabase >
```

mydatabase_backup.sql
```
```

After executing this command, you will be prompted to enter your MySQL password. The result, `mydatabase_backup.sql`, will contain all the SQL commands needed to recreate your database, including the creation of tables and the insertion of data.

Options for mysqldump

- `--single-transaction`: Ensures a consistent snapshot by wrapping the backup in a transaction, enhancing performance for InnoDB tables.
- `--routines`: Includes stored procedures and functions in the backup.
- `--triggers`: Exports triggers associated with the tables.
- `--no-data`: Backs up only the schema without the row data.
- `--databases`: Allows backing up multiple databases at once.

Example: Creating an Incremental Backup

While `mysqldump` does not directly support incremental backups, you can create a logical backup of data changes manually. First, ensure binary logging is enabled in your MySQL configuration by adding the following line in your `my.cnf`:

```ini
[mysqld]
log-bin=mysql-bin
```

After enabling binary logging and making the necessary changes, you can take a full backup and then periodically dump the binary logs for later application to a restore of the full backup.

Example: Backup Scheduled Using Cron

To automate your backups, you can use cron jobs. Here's how you might set up a daily backup of your MySQL database:

1. Open the crontab configuration:

```bash
crontab -e
```

2. Add a cron job to run `mysqldump` every day at 2 AM:

```bash
0 2 * * * /usr/bin/mysqldump -u username -p'your_password' mydatabase > /path/to/backup/mydatabase_backup_$(date +\%F).sql
```

The `$(date +\%F)` command appends the current date to the filename, making it easy to manage multiple backups.

Restoring Databases

Restoring a MySQL database from a backup can be straightforward, provided you follow the correct steps. The restoration method depends on how you created the backup.

Restoring from a Full Backup Using mysqldump

To restore the database from the `.sql` file generated by `mysqldump`, you can use the following command:

```bash
mysql -u username -p mydatabase < mydatabase_backup.sql
```

This command re-creates the database structure and inserts all the data captured in the backup. If the database does not exist, you need to create it first.

Creating a Database Before Restore

If the database does not exist, create it using:

```sql
CREATE DATABASE mydatabase;
```

You can run this command in the MySQL shell or include it in the `.sql` backup file:

```sql
```

```
CREATE DATABASE IF NOT EXISTS
mydatabase;
USE mydatabase;
```
```

### Restoring from Incremental or Binary
Log Backups

When working with incremental backups or
binary logs, the restore process becomes
slightly more complex.

1. **Restoring a Full Backup:** Start by
restoring the latest full backup using the
`mysql` command as shown above.

2. **Applying Incremental Backups:** After
restoring the full backup, apply each
incremental backup in the order they were
created. This typically involves executing
SQL files created by `mysqldump` for the
incremental backups.

3. **Applying Binary Logs:** Use MySQL's
`mysqlbinlog` command to apply binary log
changes. For example:
```

```bash
mysqlbinlog /path/to/binlogs/mysql-
bin.000001 | mysql -u username -p
mydatabase
```

Repeat this for each binary log file that
captures changes made since the last full
backup until you have captured all changes.

Using the MySQL Workbench for
Recovery

For users who prefer a graphical interface,
MySQL Workbench can also be utilized for
backup and recovery tasks. The backup can be
done through the "Data Export" option, and
you can restore a database using the "Data
Import" option.

Conclusion

In conclusion, establishing a robust backup
and recovery strategy is crucial for protecting
your MySQL databases against data loss.
With various backup strategies, and tools like
`mysqldump` and binary logs at your disposal,

you can customize a strategy that fits your operational needs. Always remember to test your backups and recovery procedures regularly to ensure that your data can be restored in a timely and efficient manner when needed. By following the guidelines outlined in this article, you can significantly reduce risks associated with data loss and ensure the longevity and availability of your valuable information assets.

10. Working with MySQL in Applications

MySQL is one of the most popular relational database management systems (RDBMS) utilized in various applications ranging from web applications to enterprise systems. Its strength lies in its reliability, flexibility, and ease of use. In this piece, we will explore how to connect and integrate MySQL with different programming environments: PHP, Python, and Java.

Connecting MySQL with PHP

PHP (Hypertext Preprocessor) is one of the most widely used server-side scripting languages, especially in web development. Combining PHP with MySQL is a powerful approach to building database-driven web applications.

Setting Up MySQL with PHP

1. **Install MySQL**: Ensure you have MySQL installed on your server. You can use tools like XAMPP, MAMP, or WAMP for

easy installation if you're working on a local system.

2. **Create a Database**: Using the MySQL command line, you can create a new database:

```sql
CREATE DATABASE mydatabase;
```

3. **Create a Table**:

```sql
USE mydatabase;

CREATE TABLE users (
    id INT(11) AUTO_INCREMENT PRIMARY KEY,
    username VARCHAR(50) NOT NULL,
    password VARCHAR(50) NOT NULL
);
```

4. **Connecting to MySQL with PHP**:

To connect PHP with MySQL, you can use the MySQLi (MySQL Improved) extension or

PDO (PHP Data Objects). Here's a simple example using MySQLi:

```php
<?php
$servername = "localhost";
$username = "root";
$password = "";
$dbname = "mydatabase";

// Create connection
$conn = new mysqli($servername, $username, $password, $dbname);

// Check connection
if ($conn->connect_error) {
    die("Connection failed: " . $conn->connect_error);
}
echo "Connected successfully";
$conn->close();
?>
```

5. **Performing CRUD Operations**:

- **Create**: Insert new records.

```php
$sql = "INSERT INTO users (username,
password) VALUES ('testuser',
'testpassword')";
  if ($conn->query($sql) === TRUE) {
    echo "New record created successfully";
  } else {
    echo "Error: " . $sql . "<br>" . $conn-
>error;
  }
```

- **Read**: Retrieve records.

```php
$sql = "SELECT id, username FROM
users";
  $result = $conn->query($sql);

  if ($result->num_rows > 0) {
    while($row = $result->fetch_assoc()) {
      echo "id: " . $row["id"]. " - Username:
" . $row["username"]. "<br>";
    }
  } else {
    echo "0 results";
```

```
}
```

- **Update**: Modify existing records.

```php
$sql = "UPDATE users SET
username='updateduser' WHERE id=1";

if ($conn->query($sql) === TRUE) {
    echo "Record updated successfully";
} else {
    echo "Error updating record: " . $conn->error;
}
```

- **Delete**: Remove records.

```php
$sql = "DELETE FROM users WHERE id=1";

if ($conn->query($sql) === TRUE) {
    echo "Record deleted successfully";
} else {
    echo "Error deleting record: " . $conn-
```

```
>error;
  }
```

Using MySQL with Python

Python is another versatile programming language that offers various libraries to integrate with MySQL. The `mysql-connector-python` and `PyMySQL` libraries are commonly used for this purpose.

Setting Up MySQL with Python

1. **Install MySQL Connector**: You can install the MySQL connector using pip.

   ```bash
   pip install mysql-connector-python
   ```

2. **Connecting to MySQL**:

   Here's a basic example of how to connect to MySQL using the connector.

   ```python
```

```python
import mysql.connector

conn = mysql.connector.connect(
    host="localhost",
    user="root",
    password="",
    database="mydatabase"
)

cursor = conn.cursor()
cursor.execute("SHOW DATABASES")

for db in cursor:
    print(db)

cursor.close()
conn.close()
```

3. **Performing CRUD Operations**:

   - **Create**:

   ```python
   cursor = conn.cursor()
   cursor.execute("INSERT INTO users
   (username, password) VALUES (%s, %s)",
   ```

```
('testuser', 'testpassword'))
  conn.commit()
  print(cursor.rowcount, "record inserted.")
```

- **Read**:

```python
cursor.execute("SELECT id, username
FROM users")
  for (id, username) in cursor.fetchall():
    print(f"id: {id}, Username: {username}")
```

- **Update**:

```python
cursor.execute("UPDATE users SET
username = %s WHERE id = %s",
('updateduser', 1))
  conn.commit()
  print(cursor.rowcount, "record(s) affected")
```

- **Delete**:

```python
```

```
    cursor.execute("DELETE FROM users
WHERE id = %s", (1,))
    conn.commit()
    print(cursor.rowcount, "record(s) deleted")
```

Integrating MySQL with Java

Java is a widely-used programming language, particularly in enterprise level applications. The JDBC (Java Database Connectivity) API provides a standard method for connecting Java applications to various databases, including MySQL.

Setting Up MySQL with Java

1. **Add MySQL Connector**: You need the MySQL JDBC driver (`mysql-connector-java`). You can download it and add it to your project library or add it as a dependency in Maven.

```xml
<dependency>
    <groupId>mysql</groupId>
    <artifactId>mysql-connector-
```

```
java</artifactId>
    <version>8.0.27</version>
  </dependency>
  ```
```

2. **Connecting to MySQL**:

Here's how to establish a connection in Java:

```java
import java.sql.Connection;
import java.sql.DriverManager;
import java.sql.SQLException;

public class MySQLConnection {
    public static void main(String[] args) {
        String url =
"jdbc:mysql://localhost:3306/mydatabase";
        String user = "root";
        String password = "";

        try (Connection conn =
DriverManager.getConnection(url, user,
password)) {
            if (conn != null) {
                System.out.println("Connected to
```
```

the database");
```
            }
        } catch (SQLException e) {
            System.out.println(e.getMessage());
        }
    }
}
```

3. **Performing CRUD Operations**:

   - **Create**:

   ```java
   String sql = "INSERT INTO users
(username, password) VALUES (?, ?)";
   try (PreparedStatement pstmt =
conn.prepareStatement(sql)) {
       pstmt.setString(1, "testuser");
       pstmt.setString(2, "testpassword");
       pstmt.executeUpdate();
   }
   ```

   - **Read**:

   ```java
   ```

```java
String sql = "SELECT id, username FROM users";
Statement stmt = conn.createStatement();
ResultSet rs = stmt.executeQuery(sql);
while (rs.next()) {
    System.out.println("id: " + rs.getInt("id") + ", Username: " + rs.getString("username"));
}
```

- **Update**:

```java
String sql = "UPDATE users SET username = ? WHERE id = ?";
try (PreparedStatement pstmt = conn.prepareStatement(sql)) {
    pstmt.setString(1, "updateduser");
    pstmt.setInt(2, 1);
    pstmt.executeUpdate();
}
```

- **Delete**:

```java
String sql = "DELETE FROM users
```

```
WHERE id = ?";
  try (PreparedStatement pstmt =
conn.prepareStatement(sql)) {
    pstmt.setInt(1, 1);
    pstmt.executeUpdate();
  }
```

Conclusion

Integrating MySQL with various programming languages like PHP, Python, and Java can significantly enhance the capabilities of your applications by enabling you to perform complex data operations with ease. Whether you are creating a simple web application or a large scale enterprise system, understanding these connections and operations is vital for effective application development.

With the knowledge outlined in this guide, you can confidently connect MySQL to your applications and perform basic CRUD operations, setting the foundation for more complex functionalities and user interactions. Whether you're building APIs, web applications, or data analysis scripts, MySQL will remain a key component for managing your data efficiently.

11. Troubleshooting and Optimization in MySQL

MySQL, a widely used relational database management system, offers robust features suitable for many applications requiring high performance and reliability. However, like any system, it can experience issues that may affect performance and user experience. Effective troubleshooting and optimization are essential for maintaining a healthy database environment. This article dives into common MySQL errors, analyzing slow queries, and performance tuning tips to help you maximize your MySQL database's efficiency.

Common MySQL Errors

1. **Access Denied Error**
   - **Error Code:** `1045`
   - **Description:** This common error occurs when the user does not have sufficient privileges or the wrong credentials are provided.
   - **Solution:** Check the username and password being used for the connection. Use

commands like `SHOW GRANTS FOR 'user'@'host';` to check user permissions and ensure the user is correctly defined in the MySQL user table.

2. **Table Doesn't Exist**
   - **Error Code:** `1146`
   - **Description:** This error is returned when trying to access a table that does not exist in the specified database.
   - **Solution:** Verify the table name for any typos and check the database you are connected to using the command `SHOW TABLES;`. Ensure you have selected the correct database using the `USE database_name;` statement.

3. **Too Many Connections**
   - **Error Code:** `1040`
   - **Description:** This error indicates that the maximum number of allowed database connections has been reached.
   - **Solution:** You can increase the connection limit by adding or modifying the `max_connections` parameter in the MySQL configuration file (`my.cnf` or `my.ini`) and then restarting the MySQL service. Also,

consider optimizing connection usage by implementing connection pooling in your application.

4. **Lock Wait Timeout**
   - **Error Code:** `1205`
   - **Description:** This occurs when a transaction is waiting for a lock to be released before it can proceed, but the wait time exceeds a predefined threshold.
   - **Solution:** Analyze the queries involved for potential deadlocks. Identify long-running transactions with the `SHOW PROCESSLIST;` command to see which transactions are holding locks and causing the delay. You can also increase the `innodb_lock_wait_timeout` setting in the MySQL configuration.

5. **Syntax Error**
   - **Error Code:** `1064`
   - **Description:** This error indicates an issue with the SQL syntax you have used in your query.
   - **Solution:** Review your SQL statement for typos, misplaced commas, or incorrect SQL keywords. Using a SQL validator tool

can help identify syntax errors.

Analyzing Slow Queries

Slow queries can significantly impact the performance of your MySQL database. By identifying and optimizing these queries, you can improve the responsiveness and efficiency of your applications.

1. **Enable Slow Query Log**
To analyze slow queries, first enable the slow query log in your MySQL configuration file:
```sql
SET GLOBAL slow_query_log = 'ON';
SET GLOBAL long_query_time = 1;  -- Log queries taking longer than 1 second
```

This will create a log file (by default, `/var/lib/mysql/hostname-slow.log`) where you can review slow queries executed on the server.

2. **Use `EXPLAIN` Statement**
The `EXPLAIN` statement provides an execution plan for a given query and helps

understand how MySQL executes it. To use it:
```sql
EXPLAIN SELECT * FROM users
WHERE age > 30;
```

This command will output details about how the tables are joined, the indexes used, and estimated rows processed, enabling you to spot inefficiencies.

3. **Identify and Optimize Indexes**
Analyzing your slow queries might reveal that they are not utilizing indexes effectively. Consider the following:
- Ensure that columns used in `WHERE`, `JOIN`, and `ORDER BY` clauses have appropriate indexes.
- Use composite indexes for queries that filter results on multiple columns.
- Avoid excessive indexing that could slow down write operations.

4. **Monitor Query Performance**
Use tools like `pt-query-digest` from the Percona Toolkit to analyze your slow query log. This tool aggregates query log information and provides insight into the most

problematic queries:
```bash
pt-query-digest /var/lib/mysql/hostname-slow.log
```

Performance Tuning Tips

Optimizing the performance of your MySQL database involves several strategies, including configuration adjustments, query optimization, and resource allocation.

1. **Adjust MySQL Configuration Settings**
Some configuration parameters can have a significant impact on performance:
- **`innodb_buffer_pool_size`:** This determines how much memory InnoDB allocates to cache data and indexes. A typical recommendation is to set it to about 70-80% of your server's available RAM.
- **`table_open_cache`:** Increase this value to allow more tables to be open simultaneously, which Hides any latency introduced by reopening tables frequently.
- **`query_cache_size`:** For read-heavy

workloads, enabling and tuning the Query Cache can reduce query execution time significantly.

2. **Use Connection Pooling**
   Connection pooling minimizes connection overhead by reusing existing connections rather than opening a new one for each query. This technique is especially beneficial in web applications where frequent database connections are necessary.

3. **Optimize Your Queries**
   Always review and refine your SQL queries. Consider:
   - Using `LIMIT` to reduce the number of retrieved records when appropriate.
   - Avoiding `SELECT *` and only selecting the columns you actually need.
   - Refactoring complex joins and subqueries into simpler forms where possible.

4. **Partitioning Tables**
   For large tables, using partitioning can enhance performance. It allows you to break a table into smaller, more manageable pieces without losing the ability to query it as a

whole. For example:
```sql
CREATE TABLE orders (
    order_id INT,
    order_date DATE,
    customer_id INT,
    ...
)
PARTITION BY RANGE
(YEAR(order_date)) (
    PARTITION p0 VALUES LESS THAN
(2020),
    PARTITION p1 VALUES LESS THAN
(2021),
    PARTITION p2 VALUES LESS THAN
(2022)
);
```

5. **Monitoring and Analysis Tools**
Implement monitoring tools such as:
- **MySQL Performance Schema:** Utilize it to get detailed statistics about performance.
- **Prometheus and Grafana:** Use them for real-time monitoring and visualization of MySQL performance metrics.
- **Percona Monitoring and

Management:** This tool helps track and optimize MySQL performance effectively.

6. **Regular Maintenance**
Regularly maintain your database to prevent performance degradation:
   - Execute `ANALYZE TABLE` and `OPTIMIZE TABLE` regularly for InnoDB tables.
   - Implement backups and purging strategies to manage the data size.

7. **Save Results to Temporary Tables**
For complex queries that involve multiple steps, consider using temporary tables to hold intermediate results. This can improve readability and reduce complexity during execution.

8. **Index Maintenance**
Regularly review and clean up unused indexes, as they can negatively impact write operations. Use commands such as `SHOW INDEX FROM table_name;` to check which indexes are in use and which are not.

Conclusion

Optimizing MySQL performance requires an understanding of how to troubleshoot commonly encountered errors, analyze slow queries, and implement performance tuning practices. Systematic monitoring, query optimization, proper indexing, and configuration adjustments can together create a well-performing, efficient MySQL environment. Implementing these strategies will help ensure that your MySQL database operates smoothly, providing users with rapid data access and a seamless experience.

12.MySQL Glossary

1. **MySQL**:
   - An open-source relational database management system (RDBMS) that uses Structured Query Language (SQL) for database operations. It is widely used for web applications and supports a variety of platforms.

2. **Database**:
   - A structured collection of data stored electronically in a computer system. In MySQL, a database consists of tables, which hold the data in rows and columns.

3. **Table**:
   - A set of data elements (values) that are organized using a model of vertical columns and horizontal rows. Each table in a database is identified by a unique name.

4. **Row**:
   - A single record in a table, represented by a horizontal line. Each row contains data for the various columns defined in the table.

5. **Column**:
   - A set of data values of a particular type, one for each row in the table. Each column has a name and is defined to hold a specific kind of data, such as integers, strings, dates, etc.

6. **Primary Key**:
   - A unique identifier for a record in a table. It ensures that no two rows can have the same value for this column. A primary key can consist of one or multiple columns.

7. **Foreign Key**:
   - A field (or collection of fields) in one table that uniquely identifies a row of another table or the same table. Foreign keys establish relationships between tables.

8. **Index**:
   - A database structure that improves the speed of data retrieval operations on a database table at the cost of additional space and maintenance overhead. Indexes can be created on one or more columns.

9. **SQL (Structured Query Language)**:
   - A standardized programming language used to manage and manipulate relational databases. Common SQL commands include SELECT, INSERT, UPDATE, DELETE, CREATE, and DROP.

10. **Query**:
   - A request for data or information from a database. Queries can retrieve data, modify data, or perform administrative tasks.

11. **Join**:
   - An SQL operation that combines rows from two or more tables based on a related column between them. Types of joins include INNER JOIN, LEFT JOIN, RIGHT JOIN, and FULL OUTER JOIN.

12. **View**:
   - A virtual table in MySQL that is based on the result-set of a SELECT query. A view can simplify complex queries and enhance security by restricting access to specific data.

13. **Stored Procedure**:
   - A set of SQL statements that can be stored

in the database and executed as a single command. Stored procedures help encapsulate logic and can be reused.

14. **Transaction**:
   - A sequence of operations performed as a single logical unit of work. Transactions ensure data integrity and consistency, following the ACID properties (Atomicity, Consistency, Isolation, Durability).

15. **Normalization**:
   - The process of organizing data in a database to reduce redundancy and improve data integrity. This involves dividing a database into tables and defining relationships between them.

16. **Backup**:
   - A copy of data stored on a separate medium, which can be used to restore the original data in case of corruption or data loss. MySQL provides various tools for backing up databases.

17. **Replication**:
   - The process of copying and maintaining

database objects, like tables, in multiple databases that make up a distributed database system. This helps in ensuring high availability and load balancing.

18. **Data Type**:
   - A classification that specifies which type of value a column can hold. Common data types in MySQL include INT, VARCHAR, DATE, and FLOAT.

19. **Character Set**:
   - A set of characters that can be used for storing text in a database. MySQL supports various character sets, including UTF-8 and Latin1.

20. **Engine**:
   - Refers to the underlying storage engine that manages how data is stored, indexed, and retrieved. Common MySQL storage engines include InnoDB, MyISAM, and MEMORY.

This glossary provides an overview of essential MySQL terms and concepts, which are foundational for understanding and working with this powerful database management system.

Index

Unlock the power of databases with "Easy Guide to MySQL"! This comprehensive yet straightforward guide is perfect for beginners and seasoned pros alike, offering clear explanations, practical examples, and step-by-step tutorials. Whether you're looking to manage data efficiently, build dynamic applications, or enhance your coding skills, this book will empower you to master MySQL in no time. With user-friendly tips and tricks, you'll navigate complex queries with ease and boost your career prospects.

ISBN 9798342997287

9 798342 997287